# Happy Coloring!

**Heather Land**

HEATHER'S ADULT COLORING BOOKS
www.HeatherLandBooks.com

# COLOR TEST SQUARES

TEST YOUR COLORS HERE AND USE THIS
PAGE AS A REFERENCE GUIDE

# COLOR TEST SQUARES

TEST YOUR COLORS HERE AND USE THIS
PAGE AS A REFERENCE GUIDE